Weightless Word

Alfred Celestine

Weightless Word
—selected poems—

x

First published in the United Kingdom in 2017 by
Shearsman Books
50 Westons Hill Drive
Emersons Green
BRISTOL
BS16 7DF

Shearsman Books Ltd Registered Office
30–31 St. James Place, Mangotsfield, Bristol BS16 9JB
(this address not for correspondence)

www.shearsman.com

ISBN 978-1-84861-528-1

Contents

Other Poems

Confessions of Nat Turner

Preface

It is winter.
The house on Crow Street is empty.
It smells of death.
It is stuffed with incident.
A child in rags
Descends like a hawk suddenly.
An old woman,
Her legs bowed, strips the remains.
It is raining.
She collects useless items, she
Remembers joy,
Remembers how he ate hard bread.
The sun falls down
Without grace: and someone else rents
This house, this death.

1

Father
Those unwashed
Do not participate
Between reality and its
Report.

2

We can
Do without him.
Our heritage is not
Obscure texts.
Our humour is not
Vulgate.

3

Facts like
Locks without keys
Remain unopened.
There are other rooms, other myths
Waiting.

4

Statement:
I hunt the stump.
I question its body.
I feel disgust. The river soaks
Its roots.

5

The tribe
Of Word gathers
A few steps away. Blood
Introduces Poem and falls
Asleep.

6

Warning:
The procedure,
Like a fixer, fastens
Image to paper, but without
Rancour.

7

I move
Pure, specific.
I talk of thirsts, not light.
Who is he, but skilful fiction:
Skin, bone?

8

The earth
Alone mirrors
Vulgar crow who evokes
This image: bonds confess, bonds sing
Our blues.

9

Dark man
Pulls energy
From air like a wireless.
He transmits: primitive. My feet
Shut up.

10

The soul
Has its sandbars.
These days, when I stand still,
Not part of the stream, I remain
Human.

11

Midday.
The sky is clear.
The sassafrass tree sleeps
Without shame. Sometimes I can feel
Almost.

12

A crow,
Dying of thirst,
Wanders from field to field,
Reminiscing about its past,
Its droughts.

13

Jacob strums
It's doing what must be done
And keeping up appearances
To become a part of what is.

The stars are hysterical with green omens.
The wide water parts, and he slips
Further and further down into perfection

Because song is naked, and terror
Because it's organic, because it's rooted
Spreads deep into our bowels and cannot be sung.

It does not have a name this tune.
We have nothing to cleanse our wound

When a string breaks with its own song.

He sees pilgrims, horrific puritans,
Lost, like a crow flying beyond its field.

Doubt ripens.
Doubt sleeps in the mouth of rivers.
It has the colour of mustard greens.
It has, of course, two sides;
They sway within us like complaint.

Who wants to translate suffering, and who
Weeps for your old juju man now?

Here among hot ash each generation
Like smoke searching for its gone fire
Rises to tell us what we want.

The narrow gate closed.
The yard filled with enraged masters.

Dead Eye harboured horizons.
His face loomed in the half-moon.

There were rumours of owls.
There were pockets of blood.

Red cauldron of ignorance boils
Over with screams.

The crowd was like small white teeth. Standing there,
Digesting their own sins,

They spoke of refusals,
The necessity of remaining pure.

The flame grew hungry; the rope bit
Savagely into Dead Eye's wrists.

Hundreds of things connected them.
Fear divided.

The past was a bull's eye:
The beginning, the end.

They heard something approach and stop.
The tar smiled; the feathers snickered.

Dead Eye stood still.

He cut from each defeat a thread.

He emerged
A black phoenix

Intoxicated, sinister.

15

Water is the element of black bull:
Half-beast, half-man.

It was trapped in a wet labyrinth.
Its mother opposed the past.

Shrieks, prophecy.

Fallen, it escaped sordid fables.
Her body rented in two spheres.

It pulled broken plough for years. My name,
Its babel, earth.

Me: half-literate and ferocious
Hibernated.
The cold fire of this page considered
Ash, its coherent
Message failed to convince us
And rekindled doubt.

Roots clutched blind routines, halved my limbs
And lay grinning.

Old beast, with a pocket full of peanuts,
Paced alone.
Thought of waxed partridge wings, then called
Back dead memory.
The river wound past its mud hut.
Black birds like rain spoke.

I dream the dark once more, the moon
In Gabriel.

16

Then Mattie, as she was crossing corn fields,
On the road to Jerusalem, died.

The years between hope and despair
Suddenly opened, and images
Poured like rain.

Perhaps the ripe pomegranate.
Perhaps the rock partridge
Lifted the weight

And rooted, broke slowly into flower.
She conjured her life
Cruelly inarticulate.

He touched them.
How did he know these things?

A moving dark,
Crawling like a spider,
Healed their wounds with herbs.

A wild ass in barbaric Babylon
Wandered thirty years belted by death
Before he perfectly

Walked into his own ambush.

Was he the One?
The black bull, the handful of pure water?

Mother waited for the master,
Full of the ways of God,

Her feet were hungry for revenge.

17

The earth has no place for the yeast
Of imagination.

It is a place of poltergeists.

And again: Big Mama in whom the Lord
Sang now and then like a magpie,
Testified,
Rolled in red dust of the threshing floor.

Shut in, behind the bars of sanctity,
We stamped, like livestock, common burdens.

In the dark of the sun,
Like Pasiphäe, with the same conviction,
She danced the Holy Ghost and moved
Down the line and shouted.

It was an unbearable memory.
It seemed like a vulgar dream.
Terrified,
My teeth throbbed with the treachery.

I entered
The fairgrounds of indifference.
I scratched the hard earth,
Lowered my head and waited.

I ran barefoot.
I rolled in red dust laughing.

In my grandmother's house
I forged weapons and another face.

18

Because black bull rose in a bronze wave,
Or the moon waxed red in harvest sky,
Or today in lost water, in wounded
Harbour he heard the song of slave.

Because we wait, because the sea swelled
With exhausted meaning, because once more
It beckoned Moses, and it lisped
A Promised Land lies north of us.

Shut down was crude machinery of sea.
I thought of Dead Eye rinsed in hot tar.
     I hung up the tortured hoof
     Of our slaughtered history.

Each of us still prays with the same fervour
And each of us shall lower in silence
A straw basket stuck fast with pitch.

Everything was to house disaster.
All his life was a slow migration
Mingled with dispute and bitter rain.

Who will lift this basket out of darkness?

Yesterday as river talked,
I saw unbounded light,
I saw it caught in the canebrake,
I saw a solitary man
Who could shatter the law.

19

A flock of black embers flew past
Like frigates in search of an empty berth.

I was sleeping, hidden
In Dismal Swamp. Blue wind

Hurricaned voices
As clean as bleached bone.

Hope dripped from my eye.
Before dawn it dried.

The sky had no journal
For me to study its wild solitude;

Its soul below the earth
Was palsied like flame.

It told me a secret.
My aim was to escape

And gather the lost herd.
When master could not find a trace,

He resigned himself to my passing.
Despair filled my veins with red-toothed hatred.

Its foam sucked my woman's womb.
It's there sucking, the swamp

Discharged spirit of a broken spade
Digging out alone at night stubborn earth.

In my poverty was my source,
An African peacock strutting in chains.

I felt wet roots of my dead cradle me.

20

Who thinks of the middle passage these days?
And their bodies like poisoned fish?
Like broken shards of a primitive urn?

 Ibo sounded Ibo.

 We stood in the midst of a death
 Pageant. Ardent pagans

Without a golden calf to blame.
A strand of ancestors
Hung Africa around our necks.

This secluded island

Was a run down dance studio.
We stood before mirrors.

We performed a sacred dance
On this most narrow block.
A few technical points, they said,

Ibo cut a mean step.

Pride was a more difficult waltz
Than they could imagine.

We turned once more to the sea.
The water brought us here.
The water will take us away.

He struck the sun from our eye, struck
Crescent moon strong in its song, sand-bagged
Rivers, and in the soil of his body
Bloomed another text: the sky.

Epilogue

Green bayou moans and mother
Coming from pregnant water smiles
Hard pews, mosquitoes,
Shanty-towns, joys
Red beans, sharecroppers
Dreaming of forty acres, of rest,
Plowing fields to plant cane.
I watch smoke curling between pecan trees.
I watch an old woman sewing.
Herself, a miracle.
Her eyes house experience,
Her mouth, the judgements.

    Wade in the water
    Wade in the water children
    Wade in the water
    God's gonna trouble the water

        Shout lordy lordy
        Shout keep on keeping on

            Wade in the water
            God's gonna trouble the water.

  Shout
        the blood's voice
        in its shipwrecks
        in its stigmata
        bleeds salt water

        and wanders
        a mile from the gate.

Shout

> a broken rib of moon
> pokes through palms
>
> screaming
> lethargic sea
>
> delivers its death
> its cargo of white chameleons.

Can I get a witness?

> Factories spring up
> along black coasts
>
> and business booms.

My mother cries out
A mile from the gate

> the sky has gone dumb
> its blue eye stutters in confusion

there
the dark perfume of branded flesh

there
rabid manacles sink iron teeth

there
syphilitic slavery cripples me
deforms bone of my bone
and its cankerous dream
is the mark of Cain

there
the sea changes

       cries
       forget forget
       repeats and repeats
       forgive forget forgive

       cries
       I am on the wrong side of death

       cries
       America looks like water moccasin
       swallowing a catfish.

I watch. I hear.

I chant silent stars.
I chant cracked shell of Brer Cooter.

The things I heard
When I didn't have a gun
And in the depths of my heart
Without a shadow, without a name
Without a god, without roots, without hope
                          I become a medium
And the dead plunge their voices like needles
In my veins and speak through my blood.

A turbulent rainbow arc:
Its black bottom burns
            past marrow and mother
            past jails, past welfare lines
                     past fire.

Passing Eliot in the Street

Absence

I will not answer when he calls
even if he coos *I missed you* :
particularly that.
Even in expectation of something
extraordinary, circled
in celebration on the calendar,
but disregarded:
I missed you
entirely draws up, adjusts,
soft re-alignments of self
coming true.

I am sick and tired of trees, of stars
who, one by one, on arriving in the sky
dare me to wish for anything.
In any event, he's gone with another woman –
that one, smiling beside me,
on the right bank of the Seine
in the holiday snap.
In another one, taken
from his wallet, evidence more wanted
was apparent: it now lies discarded.

I remember my mother had told me
...what lasts is what you start with...
I look into a mirror
he hung
in the hallway, lopsided
thinking
                    Nothing...
                    I am nothing...

In my body, I felt no pain,
when he left
and chatted away to others.

Women, easily
nursing the humiliation
of being abandoned,
say *I am going forward to a different life*
my white dress billowing and showing glimpses.
Though nothing else much is going on,
because it is our anniversary,
my single name comes back to me
like his promise *until death do us part.*
I understand there is nothing doing,
except the clock glows and the windows glow,

his voice becomes vagrant; it tramps
absence to absence, woman to woman:
all the furniture strains
to utter the very instant
I had no place to go,
save the site of my unhappiness.

So there it is. Nothing much else needs
be said really. There is no deception
anymore: what can be said for a man
who understands me better being abroad.
I shall be the earth and he
shall be a silence
in the earth.

I shall breathe in deeply
the half light
of the house we shared,

shall breathe out all the stale
odours of his body.
My breath weeps
his name; my hands draw in the air
the name of his aborted child.

In the broken pot
of marriage
plants are born:
the brilliant woman rooted within me,
brilliant, culminated,
cowed now,
cowed.

Self Definition

I am no Socrates.
He speaks to me of many other things –
of memories and yearnings,
of things which he never proofed.

I am no Plato.
I think with my eyes and with my ears
with my hands, with my feet
with my nose and with my mouth.

I have never done as much thinking.
Charles and Steve have, and they have
philosophies and purple prose reports.

If they appear to me as trees and houses
and streets and horses and birds,
it means they want me to know them
as houses and trees, as horses and birds and streets.

The angel, Eve and Adam escaped,
Jehovah stopped dead in his tracks.

He stands before the gate to this day –
a symptom, a hospice, a lighthouse
warning me off all knowledge.

That I have seen them is all there is to say.

In the distance a hawk circles overhead;
when he cries, I put out a slab of meat.

In a nearby field a Clydesdale canters;
when he neighs, I drop three apples.

The things to see are infinite.
Those to say, few.

Between there and the year of their deaths
I look and I am moved.
I am even at odds with myself –
unsatisfied, making out
boundaries of my own life are scuffed.

I am experimenting,
leaving them, experimenting,
finding no-one can satisfy me.

Charles and Steve have come
alone; all the voluptuous
sweetness of their dead bodies
fills the houses and streets
of my being.

This is bitter enough:
syllables of shadow, and leaves
sullen with mud, and shoes
in wiry grass become their wills.

I am no Socrates.
I am no Plato.

In me, evening falls
as memory on water
widens its rings.
I am alone, and only pretend
tomorrow's another day.

A Walk in Winter Rain

If men were as much men
as lizards are lizards
they'd be worth looking at.
                    D.H. Lawrence

This poem has a pain worth looking at.
Its best lines wake at the crack of daybreak
carrying the wastes of night to the page.
Each stanza when I look at it is slowed –
the thought having been picked clean of passion;
the feeling swiftly translated and stacked
in rough drafts so that you will come to it.

In this insanity volume grew
without grip or focus or tenure –
the defeats, the longing to find
another cause to survive is the rim
of some galvanised memory; touching, passing
only the aftertaste of want,
of the lives growing out of its life.

I arrive late. I timidly open
the one closet I know and step inside
peering out at the rope-off room for you.
Familiar smells of all that's male make me
look for language on the cruel surface
of a broken mirror; it catches my absence
in surprise; it reflects no feeling on which thought
stands fast.

The fever of my pace on a walk in winter rain
listens again for particular notes; Amy Lowell sees
a grove of olive trees, sucked against the hillside,

grow frosted with the terrible beauty of birds
grubbing for worms, panhandling for some bread.
I allow this meeting of love and lumber
in an oasis of private meanings.

The trees newly loved by rain, the lizards sunning
on the backs of benches, quietly peruse me:
normal men with the accepted mores and norms
fill the air with apathy and disgust.
I know myself – unremembered and alone.
Alone before a silent dictionary.
Alone before the birth of my own male voice.

Call Me

The simple weight of all I was survives
in distress, in the silent posturing,
in voices – orphic and marine – and want
whales erotic sonnets unwilled, resigned.
I wake to watch a stranger's face, and hands –
without any sense of the *infinite*
fraternity of feeling – pull alone,
pull on an absence in your eyes, and find
things stalked in vain, things asked: bread of my flesh,
do you want to be broken up? Or fed
many silences and sanctified things
felt to make fugitive this guilt outcast?

"*The true mirror of life – procreation –*
will not have us in its glass," you said, fearing
I'd wake to watch the man I loved, above all
others, melt away in a marriage,
in love become other and not himself.
The simple weight of all I am matters
and lifts lofty words, and turns on what man
must do; on what God or on what St. Paul
thought wrong to do. Love wins over us: stripped
of the jealous redness of eye, of tastes
learned from normal practice, I am saintly
in body and soul, aware of the loom
of love, and pray for a swift reunion.
Green tales and triumphs have no intercourse.
Death does not orphan me under the feet
of grief: no memory is trampled here.
I wash the wounds. I dress the angry cuts.
I turn on the soft afternoons, the deep hurts

and stops, only to admire what you were.
I cites the losses. I cites the power
exercised, and embrace you in parts; still,
some deeper knowledge found only at death
floats on a carved coffin, floats on: call me.

Fable

When he takes off his sock
soft ash falls from his foot.

He would come
in straight lines,

Without daylight
to a darker place.

Words have little use.
He must be accepted as he is.

You are unnecessarily afraid.
You know the story by heart.

He could have been the mouth
in the neck of a crane.

He could have been the hand
in the vein of a pony.

He could have been the heart
in the antennae of a butterfly.

He sleeps in the grove,
grows tired of suggestion

And the smell of eucalyptus.
He desires

The bud of Hyacinth,
the curve of Narcissus.

He wants to devour flowers,
to dry slugs into a fine powder.

His room,
full of chewed stems,

Smells desperate.
I do not like to leave him

Simply as if nothing happened,
As if a storm is coming.

Passing Eliot in the Street

I am ivory
coast and refusing to play
the ebony keys.
Behind an old tune it starts
with one armchair, two soldiers

starts in a belief
one holds and two must follow
detail by detail:
passing Eliot in the street
I saw green on orange.

Brown leaves of paper
fell and fell into my hands.
How many times must
I rake the words together
and set light to what I wrote?

How many drafts would
ever permit me to watch
myself arriving?
Tell me green leaves of paper
fall and fall into my hands.

That boat on the sea,
that boat without oars, that boat
before me has been,
used or not, an albatross
at the blue point of collapse.

I saw John jumping.
I knew Arthur had the pox.

Row boy   row   row boy
           a single word that reaches
           into someone's life hears

           a single feeling
           so close to death and reaching
           row boy   row   row boy
You have the anatomy
You have the spirit   you have

I saw Lorca lie
Dead on the Falls Road, and five
heard bullets (not four)
enter his body, and three
angels (not two) came, and one
English marched off, marched

down, marched upon the Falls Road –
           left right left right left
           cold light cold light cold
           'at five in the afternoon'

           'It was exactly
           five in the afternoon' when
           the nurse woke me.
– Are you feeling better now?
That boat on the sea is gone.

The armchair is gone.
The two soldiers and Lorca
dead and Mile End Road
at five in the afternoon
oversees life…   row boy   row

Inez Writes in Twilight

She flung my ring upon the floor,
Exchanging scorns, and went her way.
But I have tarried day by day
A cast-off lover by my own door.
                              John Crowe Ransom

April Year One

October: all day long
the tree outside my window
looks unwell, and leaves
a sickly yellow sail down
on strong currents of wind.

All day long the sun
whoops and dances in my room.
      The rain has stopped.
      I cannot bear her pain,
      her soft adulteries of being.

      I draw on some thought
      at her altar: loneliness
      prays without caution,
      brings her to an intense pitch
      not at all matching my own.

      North east south and west
      her fixed stone of lust I keep
      all in alcohol
      and our secret is language
      and our downfall is in love.

All day long I suck
her fixed stone, and others see
the beauty of us;
others with nothing to say
put fingers into my mouth

put thoughts into her
and the beauty disappears
and the stone turns to dust:
    the tree outside my window
    looks unwell; leaves

    a sickly yellow
    sail down: all in alcohol
    the beauty of us
    and our secret is language

and our downfall is in love.

April Year Two

She came looking back
at the edge of things she saw
    angels and demons
and if I laid hands on her
it was salt on bread   it was

looking back she came
on the verge of belief in things
    human and naked
and if I laid hands on her
it was salt on tongue   it was

unmaintained as days
when sin had its light sponsored

when she ate my heart
and if I laid hands on her
it was not in love   it was

my choice and her loss
when my own inner being
        spun out of control
she did not pause to listen
but came looking back   it was

in my heart a thorn
and if I laid hands on her
            at least let me say
in a terrible happiness
I wish her the courage

April Year Three

In a hollow   words
between us were stolen goods
            when it is not rain
        it is wind   when it is not
        door   it is a pane of glass

when it is not light
it is moon   when it is not
I am receiving
stolen goods   it is I am
not the best word   but taken

April Year Four

We followed the guide
going early to the place
for a change of scene:

            – Take the winding down of love
            and it can become once more…

In her solitudes
the past will never be passed;
in secret places
lives will cross one another:
            – Take the winding down of love…

I walk in full light
able to call on reasons
her heart eyes hands know.
I ask for her forgiveness
            – and it can become once more.
That is not to be
enters her every gesture.
Just as we cannot
close up the wounds the past makes,
we cannot keep on singing.

It does not matter;
she knows nothing will happen.
Twice I tried to say
no one dies of spring fever
and yet happiness was there,

went without saying
It was a mistake, Lucy…
it is a mistake.
The day slowly had filled up
and when evening returned

only one image
remained: a quiet woman stood
alone, patiently

on the platform,
pulling off an invisible ring.

Statistics

I am content with my lot
After all by the laws of probability
I shouldn't be here at all
                        Jaroslav Cejka

Make me swear hotly
I am content with my lot…
      this is a great scene
      words as fluid as a fjord
      fill the ears of my woman.

      She postcarded some
      statistics which revealed
      obvious details
      like the small girl who all day
      saw who she was and described

      my woman as kind,
      unmarried, and not being
      silly, simply asked
      Would you marry me? Would you?
      My woman laughed   yes   yes…

Make me swear hotly
I am faithful to my lot!
      the small boy upstairs
      is an open memory
      who tore open my presents.

      Are you a witch?
            No, for that I am the wrong sex.
      Well, what are you then?
            The man who lives underground.
      No, you live right below us.

Make me swear hotly
I am faithful to my lot!
  the mother indulges
  el niño en español
  "Give the man a kiss!"

The small boy flashed teeth.
The mother's cheek flushed out things.
  un beso, uno…
  "Men do not kiss each other;
  they only shake hands, Mama."

I hold out my hand.
The small boy, almost five, shakes;
  makes me sweat hotly
  to be constantly loyal::
  leaving, I laugh: statistics.

Fragments from the First Book of Bloods

It is late November –
              in this brilliant crevice of a room
              thirsty manuscripts of the Thirteen Bloods
grow cold and frightened; they hide and seek the spleen
of Time's unending work, unending complexes.

It is mid-December –
              here boarded up windows
              peer out of blinded panes:
because hope blackens bird song, I can read breathless raindrops,
frozen on their weather-warped frames.

It's another State of the Union day –
              wind addresses a whole assembly of staff trees
              on the whiteness of the soul, on signatures of snow.
Perhaps my purchase on time is overdue: being inside
this beautiful pendulum room, I oscillate.

Between the awakened and the sleeping shadows
              late November reigns, and for another year
              in this room, I do not move or approach
the still resemblances of exiled experience; other
places of linked contacts light up the pebbles in my mouth.

Memory seizes me and drags off luminous faces –
              faces dressed as Olorun, as Shango,
              as other names I alone stay writing.
Thankful to be spared from the joys of the human
sacrifices passing noisily amid the abandoned gods,
              who contend that mortal clay and water
              is always selfish, is always preying.

Olorun no longer exists.
Shango is a leading brand name.
The household gods are loss leaders.
      I discern the neck of a brown river
        boarded up with stones – gray, blue and ochre.

I agree to do all the tasks the gods have set: agreed,
I set out the weather: in the coolness of time I freed
many black and waltzing matilidas from the red soil
of Georgia; the gods had rubbed their palms with oil;
they have decided to be more cross-denominational.

My own thought stretches this flimsy rope-bridge
over the abyss of language, and time is a void.
Because I did not attend the wedding of Erzulie and Ham
I feel my eyes translated night into night as stars.

Maia reappears; I present her
the ewe my father was punished for slaughtering.
I no longer believe in the Shining Omens.

It's late April five thousand years before –
      "Jesus is the first pin-up boy of the Jews" [1]
      I overheard two Nigerian gods sparring.
I am empty. I hear you sobbing in the shadows,
hear the broken hyacinths pleading,
pleading for a piece of sky and many clouds.

I fish one reason out of many disappointments –
      to be immortal is my spur. Hermes' laughter draws
      the broken panes of the window together.
Innocent flesh falls from my bones.
I am transformed into a new planet:
still without a crust, undiscovered.

[1] *Line attributed to the Nigerian poet and playwright, Oladipo Agbolouaje*

In the Key of C:
Kennington Park, 24 June 1989

A minim in music
is double crochet, and when
a downward stroke of pen
occurs, it doubles art.

Unpack me piece by piece;
remove all the straw; read
all instructions agreed
before, and assemble

The words received today.
Always keep this thought out –
I do completely doubt
ends here, and will be left

To a kind of person
almost, like you, in type.
In such a mood I'm ripe
enough to be eaten

Whole.

The Letters and Numbers of Straw

(a)

…as Time runs down to its sleeping place
the darker total of Scarecrow starts
new cults of the Night flower, and dreams
flow blood-sacrifice against the Day.
Our Lady of Properties appears
in vacant lots, in empty buildings,
in trees, in stones, in flowing waters
charging us love: so when time wakes,
the mind is empty…

(b)

That night He raped her her blood ran straw.
Her mind wished nothing from the waist down
after that night and after all that
to find a scarecrow in her stomach
she became immaculate in Thought,
in Straw; the punishments, the pleasures
all filled the small sink of her wronged womb;
so when time came she squatted a field –
her name is Lookout.

(c)

I want to come back: with the secret,
with the physical poem, and link
with the deeper dream I had, and make symbols
with my own words that include all words.
Lookout smiles, but leaves her child: no ground,
no light between seasons, or darkness

with a sense of direction, and walks
in vacant lots, in empty buildings,
and the rest you know.

Who calls the lightning down?
> *Our scarecrow father would always come*
> *back home in the wee hours of night*
> *alone: out at the knees and elbows.*

Who runs upstream to source?
> *My mother bears the secret of Straw:*
> *in her breasts, oceans; in her eyes, moon;*
> *in her belly, me; in her mind, earth.*

Who spirits me away?
> *As a child, I dreamed all Freud's demons:*
> *ferocious feelings with no names*
> *as castrati. At least my hand sings.*

2.

I do not fear snakes.
The Scarecrow is my shepherd.
I shall not hunger.
I shall not thirst.

I was schooled in sex:
first women, then men & both
gave out diplomas,
but I tore them up.

Missing

You take this road; you take to other
roads: for places you want to reach are not
heard: you pause on mountain tops; you pause
on bridges, and you do not find the black bird.

Other urgencies tell its story –
moulted feathers, stones, ants and loneliness,
yellow hedges in the distance,
yellow rivers and trees,
farther on, skeletons of machines and houses.

Each cries out: *'is this what you have heard?'*
Each urge becomes voiced, and responds shyly
with a similar voice: each stills; no longer
calls for where it came from, or what it was.

Look at other urgencies in unlit landscapes
and do not walk on!
Hear how the wind will blind; it will burn,
and do not cry out!

There, within the moonlight, the hoped-for
black bird will not sing, *'I will never'* sings the black bird;
'never will', the black bird sings.

The Martyr

That's the way it was –
the toy-drum of night, soldiers,
who dressed and undressed,
in the course of their duty
a whole neighbourhood, then left

One single shoe, right
in the middle of Main Street,
we learn to accept:
our common fate that time talks
solely of small miracles.

I dream that shoe fit.
When the soldiers arrest me,
the whole neighbourhood
I am: now (lovely blinds drawn)
shuts out the noise of moonlight.

No one turns a head.
No one reads our dream or wakes
how it works both ways.
The real owner of that shoe
is dead. I am sentenced to life.

Pen Picture

In all that I knew
a cold muzzle of rain rubbed
against Eden; shut
winds rustled a memory
of grass: no word came to ache.

No word came; nothing
in all that I knew could write
the small print of things
shared or wanted: something gone
between us found agreement.

Nothing became words;
words became a pen picture
and later, we saw
a solitary moon bank
over the bare-headed trees.

"The Absence of Rice and Bridesmaids"

Four days before the anniversary
of her accident and the beginning
of another marriage stands memory.
Absences of rice and bridesmaids do sing
of permanent happiness, or stay
faithful to the night, when daffodils watched
like secret police for evidence, say,
of our real intention. And we are matched.

And what ignites some people to imagine
it's a mere convenience seem not to know
when to stop their trespass, nor examine
parts of the human condition that show
each barefoot illusion fixed in their head
is empty, is a blood vow until shed.

The Witchdoctor's Wife Looks Towards the New World

In the distance the sea crawls back and forth,
back and forth a moth flies against the screen,
against the screen where her heart is,
where her eyes adjust there is a faint light,
there is a duty to give birth to the dead,
to open mouths, quickly stripping the sea
of its African goods, of its Asian cargoes.

In the background the witchdoctor's wife watched.
Life here rests on the shore of the unknown.
The trees are as numerous as the stars;
the rivers, the slow trek of a tiger tracking
a wonderful band of migrating monkeys,
the stubborn wing-beats of bird – all push in
through an open window of memory.

In the hold of memory, events packed
together so tightly are stories lost.
Restless she sleeps and lives in a language
having no more feeling for the lucky ones
taken to the New World, taken in exchange.

History, ashamed at its silence, feels
That, with each generation, the distant
turns cautiously into the close-up.

I Am

Ben's Blackbird

When evening falls the road disappears
and again you leave us through a heart beat
the same fate: from now on our lives retreat
to trap the blackbird's song. We let the years
play with us over and over. We fall
as all poets, and become images…
earth, trees, stones, a ladder against some wall…
that makes us human: green with languages.

Mornings she walks; nothing remains to say
how the ladder as soon as it struck Grace
startled the earth, the trees, the stones. Her pace
of thought quickens – why me? The wall's a way
in my own mind to air my tongue's longing
for Ben's blackbird to make you a songthing.

More Notes Studies the Language and Meaning of Monsoon

'Having bumped into memory, time learns its impotence'.

To say I was unsettled is either to say too much
or too little: hanging on who's in the hurricane.
Still, the walk-on memories you had always feared remain
and your profession of pain was frankly quite hard to match.
I said, 'Each fact filtered through the fabric of what happened
has grudges. This conversation has little to hope for,
still less to recover. The point, of course, is not to score
too quickly a past still warm to touch. Not to have opened
something of no account, something devoid of love and future.
Not to leave silence free to gossip, or give evidence
which turns out to be less durable, smells: impotence
creates limits of language and meaning. To author
a truth which could be pickled, packed and sealed to preserve lies –
says what happens can be turned into art which time denies.'

Jestem

That certain rules are
certain ways of voice that serve –
a little below,
or a little above – you.
That certain incidents are

certain roads to take
in the town of her language.
That while certain words
completing content are: others
 were observing town-talk.

I am her door-think
in the face of a Great Bear.
Go outside the fear
in the town of her language,
stopping here and there,   without

language appearing
a daily faith televised.
Her being aware
and almost always cornered
has little to do with you –

blind and bolted shut,
surrendered in what you want,
in all kinds of voice
updating her verb *to be* –
not agreeing who she is.

I saw her country
in the village of my thought:

across the heart-page
my dead no longer can hide
my living must be speaking.

The Circus Dream

Between the night, resisting,
And the morning, repeating,
A fixed thought

Runs between rules and realities,
Runs between voices,
Runs.

You do not know what I felt:
You hear in my heart,
A man, bent over

In the background, smiling,
As he fixes the chain
On my bicycle,

Or a naked woman –
Being chased by a swan
And the local priest.

You do not see his invitation
Or smell the hot fear
In my eyes.

It ends where it starts:
The circus is turning on
Its horrors again –

Full of charming distractions,
Full of barkers.
I am the fat lady.

I am the gypsy fortune-teller.
In a red dress
I ride bare-back.

Step right up!
Kisses cost just two bucks!
I do not know on waking

My lips are bruised charities;
My hips have been used
Without permission.

Step right up!
Between the morning, resisting,
And the night, repeating,

I do not question
The truthfulness of another
Woman's body.

The freaks are gathered
At the real places, trying
Tough faces on the ring-master.

I come up, against
Endurance and false ennui,
Rules and realities.

Making myself pure
May not be more horror:
I can be the clown.

A Quiet Meditation at L'Arco near Victoria Station

I am there; beyond the first memory
certain later ones now hold up nothing.
I know the waiter feasting on Maxine's face
mirrors the minute my father found Jesus:
I knew there was no God and the stones knew
in death there comes such a clear feeling –
an opening for the free child to be
suddenly on top of the world and stress.

There becomes a space for other pastimes
for allowing the rich to get richer
for the ability to lie still in tall grass
as the crazy laughter of ants
carrying back a dead grasshopper
fills the ears of a dog sleeping
on the bottom of a stoop.

I have my own watch, my own weights.
I look to the nightmares ahead –
as lamps with lazy songs of orange light
as elbows of skyscrapers block out the moon
into distinct districts of the old and the new.

The dead proceed in the darkness
in order to hold and be held.
I often wonder about my own mother
descending constantly down and deeper
unending complexes, unending spells
occupy the dwelling place of my grief.
She grows angry when I push her aside to sleep.

In the heart-beat of a spade digging up
a bare plot of earth, the repetition
of headstones covering the bones of the dead
grows easier to bear. I am not sure
the old myths make any mention of me:
I am I see a flag at half-mast,
a voice waiting for air.

Weightless Word

Alive

The butchered reindeer is alive;
it rests on the ground,
the antlers are bloodstained
and the mouth is almost peaceful;
there are streaks of blood on its face,
it flows from the neck onto wet mud,
the pool is bright and fanciful
and there are brown swirls inside it
in the shape of a child's painting;
the animal's eyes are open
and I wonder how they worked?
Trap doors to the next meal,
cameras never quick enough;
I think of losing imagination,
I think of the bits of beauty
that refuse to stick in my head.

Always More Definition

This evening is too detailed
to be taken in at once;
sky reds, greys and blues
whirlpool in the stagnant light,
the glow of dusk fans down
like drama at the end of day;
clouds reduce and float away
in telescopic waves,
everything seems hollowed out
and outlined with a razor

and there is a steady count
as a windmill with three blades
clocks the view
in and out of focus
and there is one more pastel wall,
one more landscape of slants,
one more slab of physics
in the parted whole,
in the down and upswing
of always more definition.

A Crested Tide

The sea's being itself again,
a body of mist and dragging waves,
a bane to all the shoreline boats
beached like whales out of water;
they're stored motionless on trailers,
pointing at the hyperactive sea;
there are no people here, no objectives,
there is no reason to assume
death evolves from life
or a spirit can be as real
as the crested tide at Cromer.

Damning the Sea

Your mania of slapping,
soft folds, a spell of motion,
just a sorceress in a trance,
hurling your eyes and hips,
still to form, a body of shapes
mixed in the swell of moments;

foam for a molten carpet ride,
an ebbing of presence and time,
you return, slide to a calm down;
how I question the purpose,
the lap of your stillness,
your spray rages, roll of tides;

you wrapped your whirlpool arms
to pull on my swimming mother,
as I sat on sand, too young for loss,
a child in fantasy, store of sensing,
and now a fury – I set sun on you,
yell thunder down your fathoms,

I'll drag waste onto these shores,
flatten the waves, tar your coral,
you will darken in pools of oil
as I float on your churning skin,
in innocence and known wonder,
I damn you, with loathing and love.

Demons Walk from Love

I think of my mother's energy
when she prays for many people,
for a chain of fortune to happen,
her wand thinned to a worn stem;
there are times she prays for herself
when she tries to fight against pain
till she decides to ignore her needs
and push forward prayers for others.

I know nightmares from her past,
her terror fleeing the Japanese,
an escape through jungle in war;
a girl's prayers, fierce as sunlight
as it spears down from the sky,
prayers rebelling on sorrow or hurt,
when she held her dying mother,
prayers that could clear valleys,

turn Burmese jungle into neat turf
as phrases slip from the tongue,
prayers ready to stop the war
like a hand scattering toy soldiers,
prayers pulsed out and into her,
a passing from weakened friends,
prayers sent into the atmosphere,
aimed, rising as beads of hope

to vanish through the highest trees
where my mother saw a secret vision,
a sighting that she would be saved,
with a chorus of prayers reaching out

to counter fear or harm that remains,
her sense of having a lifespan of love
to repel demons and random loss,
demons that fear the giving of children.

Derelict

Gypsies and dogs
live in caravans by the river,
they blend with derelict land;
they trust in fear,
in days stone cold
and borrow hope
from ships and cranes
or giant storage tanks;
they gauge the depth
of dockyard rust
or the tonnage
of chains in the sun;
they see the purpose
of poisoned waters,
mystery in a mountain stream;
what they have
is a coil of endless action,
a mass of hours
strung between their hands;
what they know
is a frame of mind
easily sullen,
they can sup the air
like a sunken breath,
hug and curse
the bones of their life,
then drag a wish
from the roughened niche
of their hearts.

Devil's Wood

Trees, undergrowth
and some surer light,
a path of fallen leaves;
each moment is holding,
it's warm, as branches
conceal a broken sky;

child's early summer,
an afternoon drift;
chords of a folk song
fill a hesitant mind,
low notes of happening,
melody and its ground;

my steps are a pattern
to a flat broken rock,
charm or spear head,
a druid's curse stone;
I bend and collect it,
trace a ragged edge;

the canopy seals a scent
of root mould and lime,
a running of unease,
burials baking
under pine needles,
captives and ritual fires.

a tunnel of deep green
opens on a serious park,
sense of urges, ruined codes,

a couple's reclining pose;
on fissures of cracked earth
crazed moments will come.

Doll's Cannibal Friend

A cycle of same dramas
pour from the little girl
into a slim body of plastic;
Barbie's fed a cheap-talk script.

Blonde with a mane of curls,
she's still in her dumb silence;
the gargantuan puppy-fat girl
has Barbie traits on tap.

Between fantasy games
the girl barely gets older;
she'll bide her time, wise-up
into a dress size of her own;

her swoon is a play perfection,
she cooks Barbie in a tribal pan:
doubled-up, catwalk legs in the air,
a doll to consume, making you want;

seasoned with tiny accessories,
tiara, handbag and princess shoes,
the girl's growing pains stir,
too real to thicken dry stew;

Barbie is stoic till the end,
a show-off, stiff fascist in pink,
her heady smile served up
when hot lips split.

Easy Going

Life runs dry
for the old men
who stand in the shade,
they gesture and smile,
they listen and talk
with an arm behind the back,
leaning in a forward stance;
they meet by the usual tree
with branches like an umbrella,
a trunk steady as a fireplace;
a fat man has his hands on his hips,
others wear peaked caps
or jumpers over their shoulders;
a few feet away
sun lights up a bed of weeds,
it lands on a puddle
with the men reflected on its surface;
the edge is a damp patch,
it evaporates fast,
like the less and less things
that make you see red.

English Channels

People are apart…

The girl is an island,
a face with inclusive meanings;
she has too many freckles and curls,
her mouth is slung with emotion;
she's more vivid than people are,
feelings come out of her
like they belong outside, anyway,
as if the way she is
has little to do with her.

The man is a pale striated sky;
his grey hair is swept back,
a geology shows in his eyes,
there are landmarks of time,
lost years that grain his being;
his cheekbones jut through skin,
his mouth is a valley,
a movement nearing an end.

>   *Do they have clashes in common,*
>   *a gulf where they both belong?*

Equal Rights Talk, the Lost Biker

It is possible to praise
the virtues of a woman
and ridicule her in private,
choose a random behaviour
of looseness and poor logic.

> *When I kill the engine,*
> *the heat of the crankcase*
> *contacts with jean and calf,*
> *control is the boot flick*
> *locating with neutral,*
> *a stimulus of road signs*
> *cools with the lashing of oil.*

Is a value real because of its opposite,
is that why cruelty is so compelling?
Sexual intercourse is the fair beasts
in a sparring of tensile abandon;
on balance, I'm reliable and a rat.

> *The best bit is when*
> *you stop at the lights,*
> *feet planted on either side*
> *of octane in a cavernous tank;*
> *they all heed the voice of revving*
> *and you look at drivers or riders*
> *as background of a speed to come.*

See me as a delegate on behalf of buses,
infatuated with a stunning motorcycle;
why do I have incredible questions?

In truth I say my character has worsened,
on suicide and football, I'm biased or wrong.

Existence of Paint

God, what else
have I done to myself?

It is ridiculous
that I am not interested
in the hidden drift of change;
once my whole attention
was there in my love
of the motorcycle's paint,

the variance of blue glitter
in a coat under pervious black.
Now I see worn reds and greens,
the mesh and octagonal bolts
rusting on the railway bridge;
I find half-words, in spellings

on vans, billboards and crates;
in the ninety-degree heat,
a girl leans from a ladder,
guiding a scraper and blowtorch;
she burns the window frame
to reach the bareness of wood.

Flight of the Fall

He flew round the world
a few hundred times,
guiding those planes
with his eye on forever,
youth with its endless glide;

as years weighed on him
he appeared from the heights,
his worn body resisting a dive;
an officer, airman in flames,
collapsing into bits of pride;

in lost control – his fate's descent,
a hero laid on random ground;
he rests on this hospital bed
with tubes feeding functions of life,
my words address his naked feet;

through neon light, he nears a grave,
I touch a rough angel, stretched wings
tattooed on his sallow arm,
the biceps grown into slack flesh;
all I have to do is convince events

to unfold in a resurrection,
so a force is whispered
back into his failing bones,
I coax his being to breathe again,
but I can't return him to the skies.

Ghosting of Her Love

She's been down the road
of retracing him
on the lightness of gravel,
her eyes embracing
sane white lines,
deviant sprawling of skid.

She's cried the night rain's blind of tears,
met the morning air as fresh monoxide,
been a phantom hitcher postponing the crash;
she's taken the wheel on a hindsight steer,
drained the dare from his scarless neck,
slammed the speedo's eyelash still.

Gunfire of a Coward

There is no blame attached to this thing;
he was a coward from a child,
he knows the nature of his cowardice
and he dislikes almost all of it;
a safe distance from a doorway
or the sights of a vicious dog,
some length from the threat of harm,
holed-up in a false imagined safety,
his word gun slips from its holster,

he fires and fires, freely fires,
his mouth fires into the gunfire smoke,
bullets made from hurtful words he knows;
as the smoke rises, sulphur thins,
he has a fair view of a space
between him and his invented target;
the gun slides back in its holster,
he sours with a memory of his words,
he guns himself down, bleeding cowardice.

Language Line

A word like love
usually has somewhere to go,
loaded with vows and vendettas,
the platonic ride it past eroticism;
language's subterranean circus
and central station,
the amorous arch tongues
into soft shoe horns
and the word flutters
from the roofs of mouths.

Innocents say it
with signs of freshness,
disperse its romance
on a canvas of skin;
it's tamed in the talk of users,
surfers on the swell of association;
kids repeat the wisdom of posters,
their accents pulse with polluted verbs;
skateboard's made in a hammer of nouns,
some words crush with corrupted meanings.

A Metrical Norfolk

On the church tower
loss rises, anger slips,
human beings cling
like moss to the walls,
voices whirl around
in a mood of fixed opinion,
while their eyes search deeper
down through the fields,
into worm furrows, insect stiles,
while the land drains rain
and greens grow strong
in some distant range
of fells and peaks;
in a fine corner
a needlepoint of light
rides on a particle of soil
that leans on a blade of grass –
from the metrics of near to far
a scale appears for Norfolk.

Ocean Wolves

All those phrases,
worn soundtracks
still in his sour head,
a forgotten hunger,
desires plain as
a cracked fingernail
and the promise
of the next ring pull,
a novice bank robber,
tale of an armed heist,

his role with a fake gun,
night raids and brawls,
baseball bats and revenge;
when he enters a house
drums and lead guitar
pulse into his stare,
he's back in a scene
of waiting beer cans;
he cracks one open,
points his sullen eyes

at the manic dance,
as lads leap at walls,
speakers firing bass;
calm in early hours,
last bodies curled
on cleanest carpet;
Jimmy prods them
with the toe end of
a motorcycle boot,
grabs a bread knife,

loaf and slab of cheese,
heads off with a gang
to sunrise on a beach;
he spins the blade in air,
a flash of karate skills,
feet crunching on shale;
he shares out the food,
some yell as juveniles,
wail as mock wolves;
Jimmy raises a boot,

stamps through the hull
of an upturned boat;
they follow as clones,
break planks into missiles,
arms flay, hurl at the sea,
laughs in the wreckage,
turn of clouded dawn,
he slows into silence,
while day washes over,
real as remains of guilt.

Prayer for Ray-Bans

Worn solely for their
intensity of shape;
sun blazing, his arm lolls
on the car window
as he drives to her
in the hospice;
black bug eyes,

they stretch his look
into a lean conclusive stare;
there in the mind,
disease is a constant
in cold compassionate eyes;
he cares for her,
he does not completely care.

She peers through her lenses
at shapes on the edge of reach,
the birthday banners,
a carpet's wear of life,
actions shaping a theme:
gliding shoes, arms at rest,
legs variously crossed,

hands in a position
informal and precise;
a head that turns
in a chosen way,
then the length of quiet
as a moist lump of salmon
is forked into a gaping mouth;

her powers are leaving her
in a systematic killing of lights;
there's a need to filter,
narrow to a kinder place,
to hide behind her sight
and be her actual self
somewhere on the surface.

Rough Diamond

You start as
a pinprick of worth
and swell into the apple of
someone's eye, you age and stick to
people as others claw after you. Then
the glamour of contact wanes, the
cry for belonging goes, you end up
a lean spectre known to a few –
cut from the apron strings,
narrowed to a natural
point of expiry.

Rural Double Bind

Ever stroked a field?

This one is Lincolnshire's coat;
I pass my hand over its top,
the crop's windblown, not groomed,
its landness warms me,
I want it to get up
and raise its back,
I think this field could be
an earth animal moving.

Isn't that the answer
to vast serious thinking?
That your wild imaginings
dare a sane conclusion,
that you can demand
the improbable impossible
and name the day
to achieve it.

Sol Sun, Mijas Rain

Powder, marine, suspended sky,
you leave me be, you hear;
my quarrel's not with a column
of blues layered high and above
beside sandstone tower blocks;
there are those who care,
casually amused, easily drawn
to radiant seas, clarity and calm,
others who disregard, or refrain;
it's only to be expected
with failure of light and sun

there will suddenly appear
a reason for Mijas mountain rain,
cloud low on incidental slopes,
mist set in sequence with gale,
stone streets glistening, awash,
underpinning those who wander
between the lapse of downpours;
directed feet, chill of hands,
forward in this line of motion,
lanes cemented, marks on walls,
a chain of moments filling pools,

this was wanted rain, waited for,
inside a chapel, the random shelter,
maroon robes of Saint Sebastian,
bearded master, with a rod of wood;
it's free to bring your torture here,
feel a living loss, then glibly smile,
distress is welcome anywhere

as hope appears to seek its way,
belief hurts – you might as well
dream fear and thrills, sell faith
to the cursed or shining sensitive.

Yours Faithfully, Sincerely

It was a virtual tearing asunder,
a lightning strike fractured the nave,
spared the supporting temple walls.

(I remember her tempest of words,
assertive with the ritual tears;
I slammed the door of a vacuous house,
a bedroom sealed as a mausoleum).

We parted our converging waves,
our vessels flying ensigns,
broken sea-lanes trying to reform.

(I stared at the photo of her weakened eyes,
whirlpools cursed by recurrent emptying).

We declared amenable independence,
defending a clause of self-reliance;
we said that we were single beings
free to cross communal borders.

(I posted fatalism in illiterate letters,
signed one "yours sincerely";
she wrote with strident informality,
smiling pain in faces drawn on the page).

Other Poems

Fragments from a Time-Table

Each day the weather gets a little colder
and the thought
that you have become a stranger
seems part of the climate.

Each night becomes a blind tenderness of trees
and the heart
that pushes aside memories
seems part of the daylight.

Each day and each night need no-one to define
and the love
that thought and the heart combine
seems part of the future.

Freedom

The whole frame of the doorway fills with fear:
the young men emerging early for work
look back on spouses covered with fatigue;
the children have already begun
to lay aside the night and its terrors.
Afraid, very afraid, the factory lights blink on
smelling of long-contracted disappointments
and the bacon, sizzling in the pan, waits for eggs.
The morning leaves skipping down steps: alone,
everybody here repeats some routine. That's why
the two women sit down facing each other,
touching coffee cups once or twice without thinking.
Perhaps they were actually touching
each other's hands because just as I glanced
a second time through the half-opened door
nobody's there, except a deserted kitchen table
searching for something, waiting for someone. That's why
the two women hurry down the main drag, turning
slowly into a side-street – a known place, Freedom.

Flight
(For Harriet Tubman)

North Star, now full of bitterness, begins
Rigid, uncertain, to explain:

The moon steals across the river.
She lights the empty house.
She pulls down – rotting and damp – her error.

Flight was a broken clay tablet,
A bleak covenant, yet somehow necessary

Because to stand was certain death.
I am still occupied with another flight,
Another wave, another saviour.

She no longer knows what to do:
Naked, alone and formal, like some moon

She wraps her grief in a red bandanna.
She needs it for her journey to the north.
She eats a small portion like opium.

Poor woman, that injured black bird
Dying at some obscure junction is I.

Enter through the abandoned roundhouse.
Enter through the wine without a smile
As I lower my eyes in red mud.

As my feet determine the direction of flight
Enter without any sorrow.

Cataract

Gone are the separated winter nights;
gone, too, the spooning back of a partner.
The callous tree-line watches birds return
lean from long flights. Behind my back, mountains
stand up, in a density of light, that might show
something natural, or keep your real source,
unknown to me, trained in least resistance.

Let us suppose that everything is marked,
that nature surpasses human understanding.
      Various and invisible watches tick off
      seasons, tides, ages of tree and of stone.
      Various and visible snapshots partly take
      a few kilometres of bittersweet events,
      a few sweeping vistas, a few lovely faces.

Familiar, skilled with use of possessive pronouns,
let us suppose his left hand slid consciously down
and over a body he did not know well: cold water
comes to its climax at my feet, rushing between my toes.
Time times time; that morning is made of memory's dust,
of imports and exports, of manifests and almanacs:
yesterday bills everyone for ladling little problems.

With the blessedness of blindness, the self
feels unfaithful to its own self and the partner
backs off with his springs and summers away.
I am lost in thought, seeking some refuge.
I suppose an unsent letter amid papers
deliberately unfiled is something more,
is the little dialogues of doubt I still have
with my baby brother in the Mojave Desert.

The Grief of Short Roses

Tonight a slight poem came
uninvited and stayed.
It constantly fell in
and climbed out
of the same argument.

The mind sailed into its darkness.
The mind sailed in
plain speech of the mother tongue.
Only in the silence of eyes
could truth rise up.

The world does not exist
on a poet's song.
No matter how much light
it holds in its words
they do not, as you may think, carry

This moment and that moment.
Look at the grief of short roses
and watch each detail
declare what happened before.

I owe no-one confession.
You being what you are –
a silent collaborator
who comes out in the open
only to feed on medlars
and who passes,

Who containers the secrets
of your own life in mirrors

content to cast no image –
only believe in words
that turn away from themselves.

Tonight a slight poem comes
Uninvited and stays
again: it begins by saying
          Nothing pleases me anymore.
          Make sure you stay awake.

Bird Walking Weather

My thoughts are crowded with death
and it draws so oddly on the sexual
that I am confused…
                    Thom Gunn

It makes no difference to you or me
if the names of Man remain in the shade.
I have on the table a modern soul.

It may seem to have a definitive form.
It may even evolve into something unique.
But what if there was no original?

Silent, skilled in the stages of science,
I, on the very brink of suffering,
become increasingly improbable.

I chatter on Ohm, on the ocean's springs,
on inbred vocations of trees and stones,
on ordinary disorders of rain.

I scan the best minds of this century.
I expect miracles. I am guarded
by the faithful silence of what you know.

It makes no difference to you or to me,
already convicted, confessed as poets,
if parents and grand-parents are exposed

as monsters and saints. It makes no difference,
if, in bird walking weather, I end up
under one of the many umbrellas

of what you said. Sunk in *"there's no danger"*
drowns us, discards the disguises we don
without knowing why. I sign in rain

the night sweats and sweats: shame will always be
and it must not madden, for morning's sake,
the moment we came to know there's no other

path for us to take. I no longer hear
machined words, or even console myself:
time alights between struck dead and bad luck.

Anting

Her keyhole whispers
nobody knows   nobody
knows   whispers know me
        know me know me… anioly
        ominous and beautiful

        against the falling snow
        had her had her had her… treeing
        what fear she had.
At the top of her voices
I sing against nobody.

    We are not angels
    because life does not supply
    enough happiness.
    We are not angels because
    love itself sleeps in our wings.

Her **nobody knows**
nickel-and-dimes what we had.
Nobody knows nests
in anything that might poison
anything that might prove

in her kiss, her word,
in all her riches of heart,
there was an adder
there was a distance between
what we both wanted.

There was no future
for both lives: so she climbed down

and found open roads
found avenues, found hope and trust
found me wrong. From what I'm told

she found the small lane
called Marriage-and-Forgetting.
          Now it all looks like
          long hours alone and her he
          supplies sometime happiness.

          I write to see her
          because I must say I do
          not love what must be.
In answer come back her wings
offhand and crawling with ants.

Her Reason

The broken flagstones,
the deserted square, the moon
were later reasons:
when the first drops of dawn fell
she actually was crying.

This rose which was cut
from the garden of her veins
hoped for a fine vase:
no doubt the green plastic pot
of my body did not please.

Imagination
at wit's end spreads its sad wings:
I am tied to time
night and body rising, rose,
fell down in a heap.

She'd opened herself
like a wound; fat drops of blood
peered from the whiteness
of these freshly laundered sheets:
the deep truth is imageless.

It rained. The earth dressed
and became naked. I'm now
a despised flower,
raked with dead leaves for burning:
her leaves oxidised me.

Afterword

Alfred Bernard Celestine Jr. was born on the 3rd of June 1949 in Los Angeles, California. He permanently left the U.S. around 1975 and went to live in West Berlin; he came to London in 1977 and remained there for the rest of his life. After a short illness Al (as he was known to friends and associates) passed away on 29th July 2009. An autopsy revealed the cause of death to be ischemic heart disease.

To these details, provided by Shane Tobin, who was Al's partner from April 1988 until Al's death, we might add that he was black, gay (as already indicated) and a periodic sufferer of mental illness. These things seem relevant either to the themes and concerns of his poetry or, in the case of his psychological problems, to the severely fractured publishing history of his work.

However, Al Celestine would quite possibly not thank me for making a point of any of this, despite his openness about his mental illness, for example. (I remember him *joking* about it at a reading he gave at The Blue Bus, a reading series in London that I'm involved with, on the occasion of his booklet *Passing Eliot in the Street* appearing from Jennifer Johnson's Nettle Press in 2003.) John Welch has stated that when he published Al's magnificent sequence *Confessions of Nat Turner* (The Many Press, 1978), Al asked him not to say anything about the fact that Al was black. (See 'Al Celestine', *Fire* no. 32, 2010.) I suspect this was a matter of not wanting to be pigeonholed as a "black poet" (or similarly as a "gay poet") rather than regarded as *a poet*, without any qualifications. I take the point, while still feeling that a little sense of context may be helpful to the reader.

When I published Al's posthumous pamphlet *I Am* (Kater Murr's Press, 2010), Christopher Gutkind and I organised a memorial reading and a launch of the publication, at a pub in Camden Town. It was a measure of the respect with which Al

Celestine was held as a poet that Jeff Hilson, John Welch, Keith Jebb, Jeremy Hilton, Stephen Watts, Richard Leigh, Jennifer Johnson and Peter Daniels all took part, as well as Chris Gutkind and I.

This present selection of Al's poetry is basically a sampling of the best of his work. As the subtitle indicates, it is not his complete poems – a rough guess would be that it's about a third of what he left behind. However, Richard Leigh and I have tried to show the range of his poetry, from the lyrical and sometimes fairly straightforward (though usually still involving twists and unexpected turns of imagery and language) to the dense, impacted and in some cases downright strange. The skewed or ambiguous syntax, the tendency to sometimes ram words together in unusual combinations (e.g. "whales erotic sonnets unwilled" in 'Call Me')… these and other techniques are at the service of a fierce, grave, yet also sometimes playful attention to matters of love, desire, compassion… justice and injustice… history, memory, myth and imagination.

Weightless Word was the title of a lengthy file of poems on a computer disk. The only thing in the file that overtly connects with the overall title is a poem entitled 'Weightless Road', which hasn't been included here. Given that Al was not a particularly good typist, the possibility exists that *Word* is simply a typing error. I doubt it. In Al's poetry words indeed want to fly, to soar, to lose all sense of weight, and of course they do… though there is also an offsetting darkness and gravity in the poems. The poetry is, precisely, in this tension.

Keith Jebb has written that "the moon scythes in and out of [Al's] poetry, sometimes reflecting, sometimes black. This stuff isn't an achievement – the word belittles it." ('Alfred Celestine: "an unreadable future"', in *Fire* no. 32, 2010.) Amen to that.

David Miller

Acknowledgements

Some of these poems have previously appeared in: *Fire, The James White Review* and *Poetry Salzburg Review; In the Family* (GMFA, 2001) and *Language of Water, Language of Fire* (Oscar's Press, 1992); as well as *Confessions of Nat Turner* (The Many Press), *Passing Eliot in the Street* (Nettle Press) and *I Am* (Kater Murr's Press). We extend our apologies to any journal editors for possible omission of acknowledgements.

The other poems were taken from manuscripts in the possession of Shane Tobin, Christopher Gutkind and Richard Leigh. The section entitled *Weightless Word* (which we have also used as the title of the book as a whole) comes from a manuscript with this heading, as stated in the 'Afterword'. The poems in the last section were taken from a number of other manuscripts.

Mention should also be made of the special feature on Alfred Celestine in Jeremy Hilton's magazine *Fire*, issue 32, 2010, which included tributes by John Welch, Christopher Gutkind, Keith Jebb, Jennifer Johnson, Stephen Watts and the editor, as well as a selection of AC's poems (including two not printed here).

Special thanks to Shane Tobin for permission to publish this selection of poems.

Notes

"The Absence of Rice and Bridesmaids": the title is from a poem by Essex Hemphill.

'Fragments from the First Book of Bloods': this poem has been substituted for 'Early Morning', which appeared in its place in *Passing Eliot in the Street*, because 'Fragments...' appears to be a later version of that poem. (See Jeremy Hilton's comment on this poem in the issue of *Fire* referred to above, p. 6.)

'Jestem': the title is from the Polish, "I am".

'Anting': the word "anioly" means "angels" in Polish.

The following minor editorial decision was made: in 'More Notes Studies the Language and Meaning of Monsoon', "perserve" was taken as a typing error and corrected to "preserve". Also, in section 18 of 'Confessions of Nat Turner', last line of the second verse, the version in The Many Press edition reads "A Promise Land lies north of us", which we decided should probably be "A Promised Land lies north of us".

Lightning Source UK Ltd.
Milton Keynes UK
UKOW03f1103240417
299768UK00001B/139/P

9 781848 615281